You Know You're a
Golfing Fanatic
When...

Ben Fraser

summersdale

YOU KNOW YOU'RE A GOLFING FANATIC WHEN...

Summersdale Publishers Ltd
46 West Street
Chichester
West Sussex
PO19 1RP
UK

www.summersdale.com

Printed and bound in China

ISBN: 978-1-84953-061-3

Substantial discounts on bulk quantities of Summersdale books are available to corporations, professional associations and other organisations. For details contact Summersdale Publishers by telephone: +44 (0) 1243 771107, fax: +44 (0) 1243 786300 or email: nicky@summersdale.com.

You Know You're a

Golfing Fanatic

When...

There is a suspicious looking dent next to the cat flap from the last time you 'put the cat out'.

The use of the number four in conversation prompts you to immediately duck to the ground.

You have water hazards, not water features, in your back garden.

You employ a caddie to carry your briefcase to work.

You think all chavs are budding
golfers, due to their passion for caps
and all things Burberry.

The phrase 'driving gloves' sounds strange in the plural.

Your neighbour two doors down returns a bucket of balls with a note attached, entitled 'Tips on Correcting a Slice'.

Your first suggestion for any get-together is a round robin.

You assume that a computer hacker is someone who is inept with technology.

You don't understand why people snigger if you use the phrase 'niblick', 'frog hair' or 'double D'.

You refuse to go to work due to abnormal ground conditions.

Your estate agent suggests expanding your property search beyond houses with 'excellent views over the 18th'.

The names of your children are Tiger,
Arnold, Tripp and Annika.

Asked what your favourite book is, you
reply that you prefer 'reading
the green'.

Your partner has to remind you that foreplay is more than just shouting 'Fore!' before you jump into bed.

You insist on going to a sudden death round if you tie at anything, even playing Scrabble with the kids.

You alone know the secret of the perfect interlocking grip.

You have a variety of golfing memorabilia, including a lock of 'The Golden Bear's' hair purchased off eBay.

The surrounding gardens and gutters of both your close and distant neighbours are littered with golf balls that have gone off-course.

You ask your doctor to prescribe
something to prevent backspin.

In your opinion every Masters Golf Tournament should be declared a national holiday.

Your son's school report says that on being asked the question 'What is four minus one?' he replied 'One under'.

Your wife suggests an exotic beach holiday, so you take her to the sand bunker at Geoff's World of Golf in Croydon.

Your kids are asking why, when
all their friends are playing on the
swings, they're working on theirs.

You simply can't stand lies –
especially sidehill.

Your partner suggests a threesome and you immediately fetch your golf clubs, hoping that you will be playing with Bob from next door.

Roy Orbison's 'I Drove All Night' starts to sound less like a love song and more like preparation for a competition.

Your favourite musicals are *Swing Time* and *Bye Bye Birdie*.

Your wife tells you it's tea time and you turn up at the table in full golfing garb, including knee-high socks.

Your accountant tells you a three-day
'conference' at the Royal Dornoch isn't
a legitimate travel expense.

You steer well clear of the shank if buying meat.

Your boss says your performance is
'below par' and you wonder what he's
complaining about.

You catch yourself raking the kids'
sandpit at the end of a day's play.

Your dance repertoire includes only one move: the Arnold Palmer shimmy.

Your children know better than to ask
'Are we nearly there yet?' after hearing
'Still have a fairway to go' no matter
what the distance.

You make your children refer to you as 'Par' – even though you're their mother.

Your garden looks like it has a serious mole problem from where you have been practising teeing off.

Though tempted, you turn down that offer of a pre-game swift pint – after all, it is illegal to drink and drive!

You always avoid cakes so that no one can say you've got a slice.

Your Halloween costume every year consists of pointed teeth and a 4 wood through your chest, otherwise known as 'Baffy the Vampire Slayer'.

Friends ask you to bring the chilli dip to a party and you immediately enrol in golf lessons, thinking they are mocking your swing.

You keep all your old socks so you can always say you've got a hole in one.

You can hear and use the term 'shag bag' without giggling.

Someone asks you to name The King's greatest hit and you reply that it was his second stroke at the 2004 Bay Hill Invitational.

You prefer to play golf traditionally and have a shot of Scotch at each hole – your game doesn't improve, but strangely you don't seem to care.

Your son tells you he has a bogey and
you proclaim him to be the next
Seve Ballesteros.

Your children think 'going to school' means watching a golf ball roll across the lawn.

You never buy a putter until you've had
a chance to check how well it bounces
after you throw it.

You think a night on 'the pull' means practising your golf swing.

You confuse people at parties by telling everyone they should see your moves 'on the dance floor' and then take them outside to show them your ball control.

You go looking for golf magazines in the extreme sports section.

You only use Gillette razors so you can have a cut like Tiger Woods.

Your kids get excited when you promise
them a retriever for Christmas –
unfortunately you aren't referring
to a puppy.

Your wife calls the clubhouse to wish you a happy anniversary.

People frequently ask if you've just got up, and you have to explain that your chequered slacks are not pyjamas.

Your wife hints that she wants to wear diamonds on her birthday; the patterned polo shirt you get her isn't quite what she had in mind.

Before mowing the lawn you put up warning signs which read: 'Ground Under Repair.'

Your New Year's resolution is to slim down – by eliminating all those fat shots.

Every year you visit the Tripp Isenhour bird sanctuary where you can see eagles, albatross and the rare stuffed red-shouldered hawk.

TRIPP
ISENHOUR
GOLF DVD

You take the parking space closest to the supermarket with the justification that your handicap is high.

You consider a banana ball one of your five-a-day.

The family pet dies, but you find some consolation in planning how to incorporate the mound of the grave into the putting course in your back garden.

You sacrifice all friendly associations
with your neighbours by using the side
of their house to practise your
bowker shots.

Your son gets into trouble at school
when he misinterprets your advice:
'Keep your punch shots low.'

Your number one philosophy in life is: visualise!

You ban your children from playing on the Wii as you're one level away from becoming semi-professional and nothing is going to get in your way.

Your best method of meeting new people is going after the wrong golf ball.

You tell your kids that they must store their bikes somewhere else because you've transformed the garage into an indoor practice range.

The only time you use an iron is
on the green.

Your partner would like to go dancing but your permanently square stance makes it impossible to participate in anything more graceful than line-dancing.

You crash your car into a tree as it is the only time you'll drive like Tiger Woods.

Your family decide to take up golf so they will see you more often.

Have you enjoyed this book?
If so, why not write a review
on your favourite website?

Thanks very much for buying
this Summersdale book.

www.summersdale.com

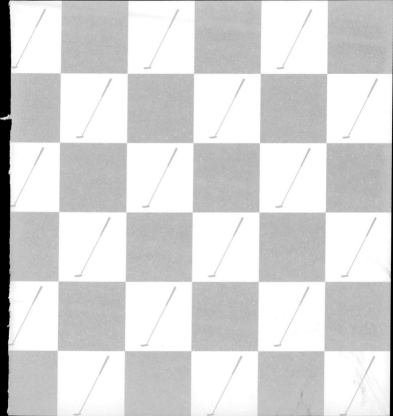